An Edible Film Odyssey

a STAR is CORN

by
**Brock
Lee**

HarperResource
An Imprint of HarperCollins*Publishers*

For Laurie, the sweetest tomato I have ever known.

For information, address HarperCollins Publishers Inc., 10 East 53rd Street, New York, NY 10022.
HarperCollins books may be purchased for educational, business, or sales promotional use. For information please
write: Special Markets Department, HarperCollins Publishers Inc., 10 East 53rd Street, New York, NY 10022.

FIRST EDITION

Book design by William Ruoto

All vegetable sculptures photographed by Laurie Eagle.
Background photograph credits:
Painet, Inc.: 4, 12, 15, 23, 40, 42, 44, 46, 49, 50, 52–56.
Zedcor, Inc.: 26-27, 38.
Sara R. Eagle: 18, 41.

Library of Congress Cataloging-in-Publication Data
Lee, Brock.
A star is corn : an edible film odyssey / by Brock Lee.
p. cm.
ISBN: 0-06-009681-0
1. Motion pictures—Humor. 2. Vegetables—Humor. 3. Vegetable carving. I. Title.
PN6231.M7L38 2003
791.43'02'07—dc21   2003042320

03 04 05 06 07 ❖/RRD 10 9 8 7 6 5 4 3 2 1

Contents

Gene Shallot

The key to Gene Shallot's success is his ability to convey the emotional impact of a movie . . . or as the Critic's Corner resident would put it, "Shallot's Appeal Brings Tears."

Acknowledgments

I, for one, thought Janis Donnaud was a bit crazy when she suggested that beyond some close friends there might be a larger audience for my vegetable creations. Without her prodding to turn the idea into a book, *A Star Is Corn* would never have been written. A big thanks to Janis for both her foresight as well as her insightful editorial comments. Thanks also to my best friend in the whole wide world, Peter Gethers, for his guidance in the ways of the publishing world and for being the best test of what is funny and what is a reach. And a special thanks to Kathy Huck for her patience with me in getting this book completed.

This vegetable-movie connection is a really interesting thing. When people would hear about the concept, particularly if they were movie buffs, they instinctively offered up ideas. Many of the movies used in this book came from the creative suggestions of Norm Stiles, Jon Korkes, Bernie Orenstein, Nicky Scharlatt, David Hayward, and a toothless Las Vegas cab driver.

The Internet Movie Database (www.imdb.com) was a tremendous source of factual information on film history. And close friends and family helped me with editorial advice, timely suggestions, words of encouragement, and movie facts. Thanks to Dominick Abel, Zig and Nancy Alderman, Glen Waggoner, Sharon McIntosh, Esther Newberg, Barbara Orenstein, Micheline and Abby Levine, Dr. Ed Kosinski, Dr. Debby Mayer, David Mayer, Judy Gethers, Joey and Debbie Helman, and Wayne and Phyllis Van Loon. And a special thanks to both Kathleen Moloney for her editorial assistance and Leonard Temko for his assistance with the images.

Thanks to my sweet Sara for not rolling her eyes too much as I was sculpting away, and thanks to her pals Marcy and Rooch, who are probably far too polite to tell me what they really thought of a book about vegetable sculpting. And I am thankful for Ben's words of encouragement that assured me plenty of other books are being published with ideas far sillier than mine. And finally, a very special thanks and debt of gratitude to my father, who taught me very early in life that there is more to the world than just meat.

Introduction

A few years ago, a simple holiday tradition began to take a curious turn. Every Thanksgiving, I would bring a simple vegetable sculpture to a friend's holiday dinner. The first year's sculpture was unsophisticated, something even a novice in the world of cauliflower and carrots could create—a turkey modeled after the Macy's Thanksgiving Day parade balloon. Noting some interest, I began to contemplate more creative designs for future presentations. As the practice developed and eventually became a tradition, the sculptures began to reflect current events or contemporary personalities, demanding a more complex design and structure. Each year, the anticipation of the vegetable theme and the lively discussion that would surround the unveiling of the sculpture became more and more spirited. In 1998, Linda Tripp and Monica Lewinsky's late-night telephone exchanges were immortalized in legumes, with details such as Linda Tripp's exquisite Napa cabbage coiffure and the stain in Monica's eggplant-colored (and, in fact, actual eggplant) dress. And the dropping of the millennium squash ball in Times Square was witnessed by hundreds of tiny new potatoes.

A strange realization came over me: I had begun to interpret the contemporary world through fruits and vegetables. Not only that, but other people were starting to share my skewed point of view. A casaba melon with two raisins for eyes *does* look like Patrick Stewart. That cauliflower *is* a dead ringer for Phyllis Diller. Ideas for future sculptures started to sprout up like bamboo shoots—use a white pumpkin for Anthony Hopkins or seven sizes of boiling onions for the von Trapp family. One after another, celebrities came to be seen as the foods they resembled. I sought relief in movie theaters but found that I no longer could see the characters, only their roots. I would blanch while watching two turnips make love. I would go to see *40 Karats* but find it extremely grating. Then the kernel of the idea for a book on

Introduction

Hollywood pop culture by way of vegetables began to emerge. No, not emerge—it began to boil and steam its way into existence.

And so began the development of *A Star Is Corn*—a reinterpretation of Hollywood's movie classics as seen through vegetable sculptures. To some this book may be as refreshing as the first bite of an heirloom tomato picked straight from the vine. To others it might seem as bitter as boiled broccoli rabe. But for all, the trip to the produce department in your supermarket will soon become much more entertaining.

Legendary Hollywood producer Saul "Solly G" Goldberg, known for closing every deal over cabbage soup at Nate and Al's.

Chapter One

Hollywood:
The Big Salad Bowl

Vegetables and movies? What possible connection can be made? Don't be too quick to dismiss the link—the vegetable/Hollywood coupling goes back to the early days of moviemaking.

In 1870, long before studios, sidewalk stars, and billboards peppered the surroundings, the area now known as Hollywood was a thriving agricultural community. Grain and hay crops were planted and harvested and pineapples, bananas, and other produce were grown and bartered with surrounding communities. Just after the turn of the century, a local agrarian discovered that generous applications of cow manure helped his crops to grow. Not so coincidentally, the first Hollywood studio was constructed shortly thereafter on that exact site, and the seeds of the Hollywood moviemaking industry were sown.

Early filmmakers like D. W. Griffith took advantage of the mild California winters and an abundance of local produce to grow the film industry. A little-known fact about two of Griffith's earliest movies is that their storylines were very different in their early versions. Griffith, an uncompromising vegetarian, felt that the eating habits of the average American were abhorrent, and his original story, *Girth of a Nation*,

was a major indictment of the nation's poor eating habits. On the advice of studio investors that moviegoers would shun vegetarian didacticism but cluster to tales of racist hate mongers, Griffith changed the title to *Birth of a Nation* and concluded the film with a scene of Klansmen on horseback waving flaming shish ke-bab skewers. A year later, Griffith bowed once more to studio pressure and changed the storyline of *Intolerance* from a tale of an eight-year-old boy who would not eat his peas to a multilayered historical chronicle of religious and political bigotry.

Yes, Hollywood really is just a big salad bowl. It's a place that drools over tasty, young cherry tomatoes while tossing away vine-ripened veterans. It's a place where more dressing is added to cover up bland and limp ingredients. A place that changes one ingredient so it can serve the same old salad with a fancy new name. And a place that, on the surface, looks healthy, but contains hidden ingredients that make you bloated. But like the ingredients in the salad, the Hollywood aura needs to be washed, scrubbed, and peeled before it can be enjoyed. Hence this book.

CHARLIE CHAPLIN
MODERN THYMES

The Little Tramp's indictment of modern society
the machine age, and dried seasonings

Chapter Two

The History of Hollywood in Vegetables

Professor Bean's Removal, starring Fatty Arbuckle, is released. The less known about the storyline of this film, the better.

The Silent Era

Many consider the silent era to be the golden age of movies for vegetables because, of course, they can't talk anyway. The seminal early silent movie was the classic *Bean Hur,* a film that set the bar for all future "sorrel and sandal" movies.

The influence of *Bean Hur* can be seen in two other "cast of thousands" movies: the 1960 Kirk Douglas epic, *'Sparagus,* and the 2000 Academy Award winner *Gladi-Tater.* The scene in *'Sparagus* in which the title character leads his fellow legumes with their handcrafted *'Sparagus* spears in revolt against the Roman army owes much to the influence of *Bean Hur.* And Russell Crowe's turn as the freed slave in *Gladi-Tater,* just like Ramon Novarro in *Bean Hur,* proves that spuds and studs make for a powerful film combination.

In every good "masked man" adventure, something always gives away identity of the lead character. In *The Invisible Man,* it's his onion brea

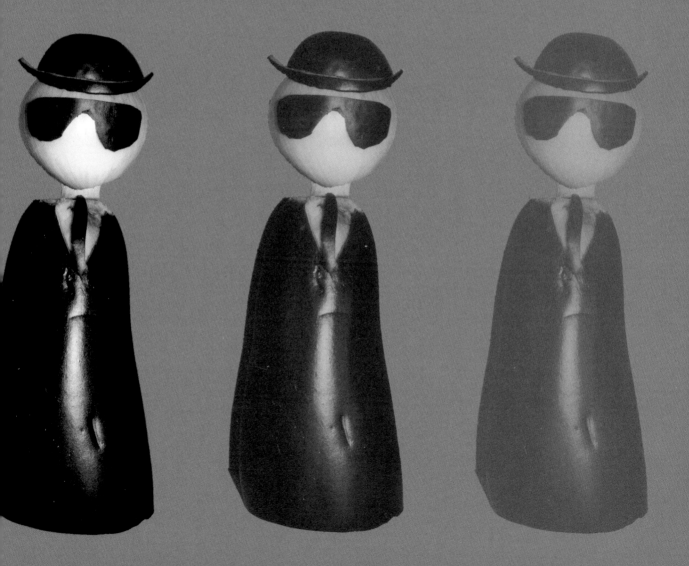

Hollywood producers employ the casting couch to "audition" starlets for their movies. Five years later, Orson Welles introduces his casting "quiche" to audition caterers for his film shoots.

The Depression and the War Years

The Great Depression saw an absence of vegetables in films because of the need to redirect them to soup kitchens to feed the poor. They became more of a daily necessity than a source of entertainment. It was hard to laugh at *My Little Chicory* when that chicory could have been part of your dinner.

While scarce, there are still a few vegetable-inspired movies from this time period. Audiences both hooted and salivated during the carrot-eating sequence in *It Happened One Night.* And they rooted for the populist title character of *Mr. Seeds Goes to Town* to plant one on the kisser of Babe Bennett, the hotshot reporter of the local newspaper.

This is the classic Steinbeck tale of the Joad family, farmers from Oklahoma w head to California in the 1930s in search of a better life. The movie ends sa with the Joads withering to raisins in the California s

a STAR *is* CORN

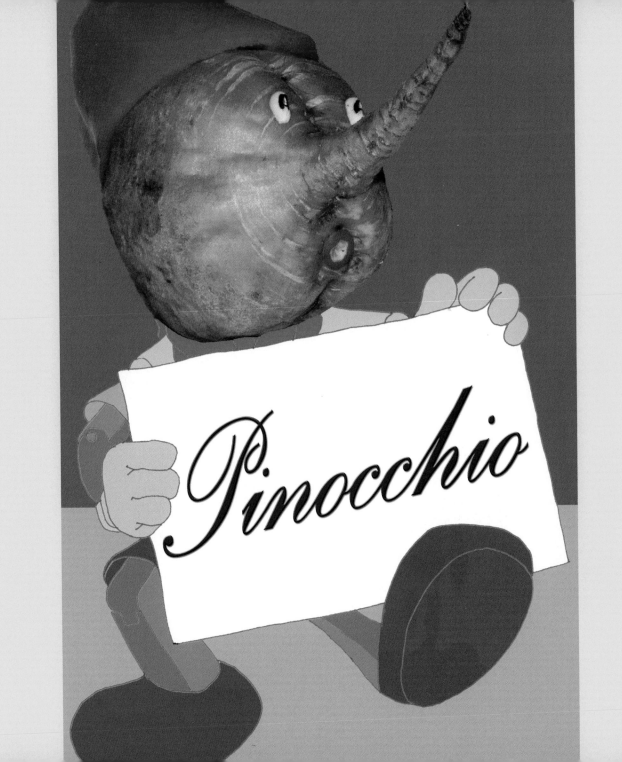

First concession stand installed at a movie theater in Joliet, Illinois. After a couple of failed experiments with peas and brussels sprouts, popped corn becomes the staple for movie theater snacks.

Finally, a love for both Shirley Temple and corn on the cob drew in the masses to see *The Little Kernel.* On the other hand, some audiences got steamed over *Of Rice and Men* on the grounds that its poignant portrayal of two dreamers searching for a better life demeaned the importance of such a valuable grain.

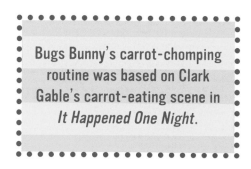

Bugs Bunny's carrot-chomping routine was based on Clark Gable's carrot-eating scene in *It Happened One Night*.

The scarcity of vegetables in film continued through World War II with the notable exception of the patriotic *Marine Taters*, starring Patrick O'Brien. To this day, it's difficult to order a plate of O'Brien potatoes without thinking about these brave soldiers. Once the war was over, movies took on a lighter, more optimistic tone. In 1946, *It's a Wonderful Life* was released and quickly became one of the most heartwarming Christmas

...en this Disney classic was released in China, the tag line ...came scrambled in translation and millions of Chinese ...viegoers were lured with the phrase "The story of a puppet that ...nted to become bok choy."

The Sands of
IWO JIMA

In an effort to drum up postwar business, theaters in Iowa release the World War II coming-home drama under the retitled name *Best Ears of Our Lives*.

movies of all time and has been translated into eighteen languages. An interesting side note is that in adapting the movie to a Russian audience, the translation of the movie's famous closing line was translated as "Look Papa, the Czar says 'Every time a bell rings, the beets are being delivered.'"

outtake from this famous World War II movie in which the ̄rines are raising the fig over Iwo Jima and singing "From the lls of Montezuma, to the stores of A&P . . ."

The AMA lauds *The Seven Year Itch* as a cautionary documentary about the allergic reaction to peanuts.

The Fifties

While many deride the fifties as an era of bad drive-in movies and tasteless frozen vegetables, a number of films with fresh ideas and fresh vegetables were still a potent Hollywood pairing during this decade. The fifties sci-fi craze generated classics such as *Plantain Nine from Outer Space*, *The Day of the Truffles*, and the poignant *Creature from the Black Legume*. The latter film explores the little known past of the Creature, growing up as a little sprout, and the disastrous accident with the pickling juice that turned him into a disfigured, misunderstood character. The Creature's sad, shish kebab ending was interpreted by many critics as a fervent plea for the elimination of cruelty to vegetables.

The actual translation of the solemn phrase "Klaatu Bara Nikto" is "We have come in pea

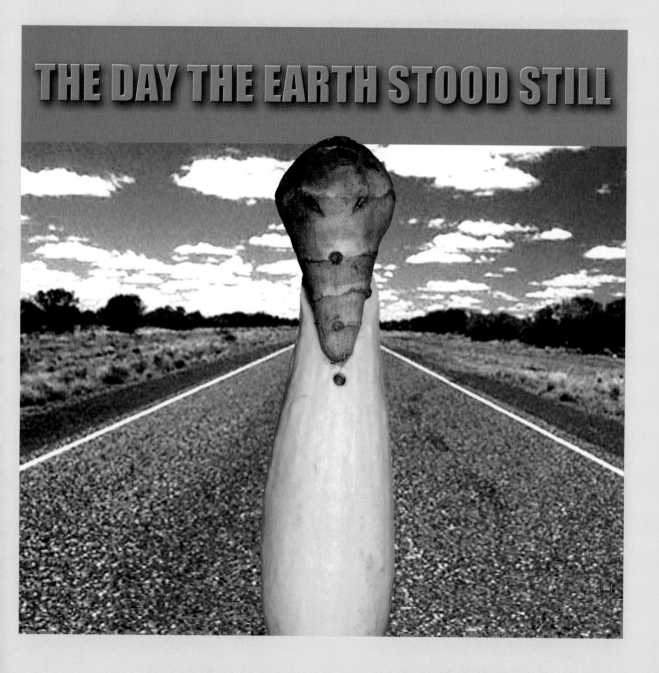

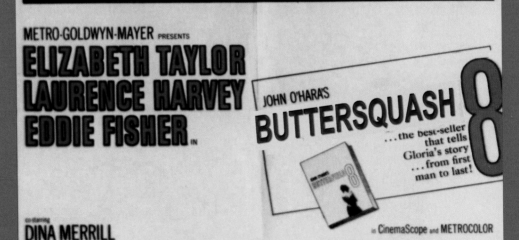

During the initial release of *Picnic*, a subliminal message of "Eat popcorn" was periodically flashed on the screen. Sales of the snack reportedly increased by 15 percent in many theaters.

The 1950s also saw the emergence of the Beet Generation, a group of poets, writers, and philosophers with a fresh approach to

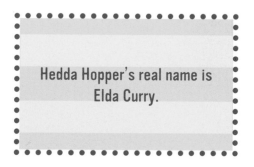

Hedda Hopper's real name is Elda Curry.

literature and a defiant, demonstrative social stance toward conventional society. Hollywood picked up on the Beet craze and through such movies as *Black Bean Jungle* and *Rebel Without a Garnish* (starring James Bean), this antiestablishment attitude was served up to a hungry audience of postwar teens.

the most desirable woman in town, just call Buttersquash 8. e will do anything for you, even deliver your groceries.

One Potato, Two Potato is released. Dan Quayle is fired from his position as the arts and entertainment copy editor of the Huntington (Indiana) *Herald*.

The Sixties

The sixties was a decade of peas and love, and a time when studio heads were beginning to recognize the appeal of vegetable references in films. Producers started to center movie ideas around a specific legume and would have writers frame a movie script around a vegetable-themed title. They would sometimes go so far as to suggest that an actor's name be changed to fit the theme of the movie. Some early ideas for films of the sixties included:

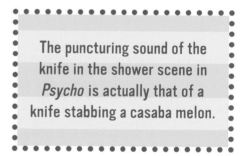

The puncturing sound of the knife in the shower scene in *Psycho* is actually that of a knife stabbing a casaba melon.

- *Zorba the Leek*, starring Anthony Quince

worst that could happen when your mother yells at
to finish all your vegetables.

19

The History of Hollywood in Vegetables

The Good, the Bad, and the Ugly is released. American Produce Growers adopt same classification system for produce.

- *Valley of the Dills*, starring Sharon Tater, Barbara Gherkins, and Patty Cuke
- *The Greens of Navarone*, starring Gregory Peck, Anthony Quince, Stanley Baker, and Irene Papas Fritas
- *To Dill a Mockingbird*, starring Gregory Peck and Broccoli Peters
- *True Grits*, starring John "Cuke" Wayne
- *A Man for All Seasonings*, starring Peel Scofield

Many groundbreaking films sprouted from the sixties. *Bob and Carrot and Ted and Alice*, for example, destroyed film taboos in the areas of both group and vegetarian sex. Early reviews ("A film that grates at the core of contemporary sexual mores"—*Gourmet*) gave an indication of the impact that this movie would have in America's bedrooms and kitchens.

This landmark film of the sixties portrays the clash of coming-of-age uncertai and middle-class values. A little-known vegetable fact is that in the original sc the classic "plastics" line was written as "Ben, I have one word for you, pect

THE
GRADUATE

Rosemary's Baby is released. The Catholic Church decries the influence of both satanism and herbs on the movie.

There are some interesting anecdotes about how various films in this decade were named. For example, *Some Like It Hot* came from an overheard order for mushroom barley soup at the Second Avenue Deli in New York City and *Walk, Don't Run* was a bad translation of the Chinese kitchen warning "Don't run with wok." And who would have known that Paul Newman's *Cool Hand Cuke* ("Anyone who loses his spoon spends a night in the crisper.") would portend Mr. Newman's later entry into the salad dressing business.

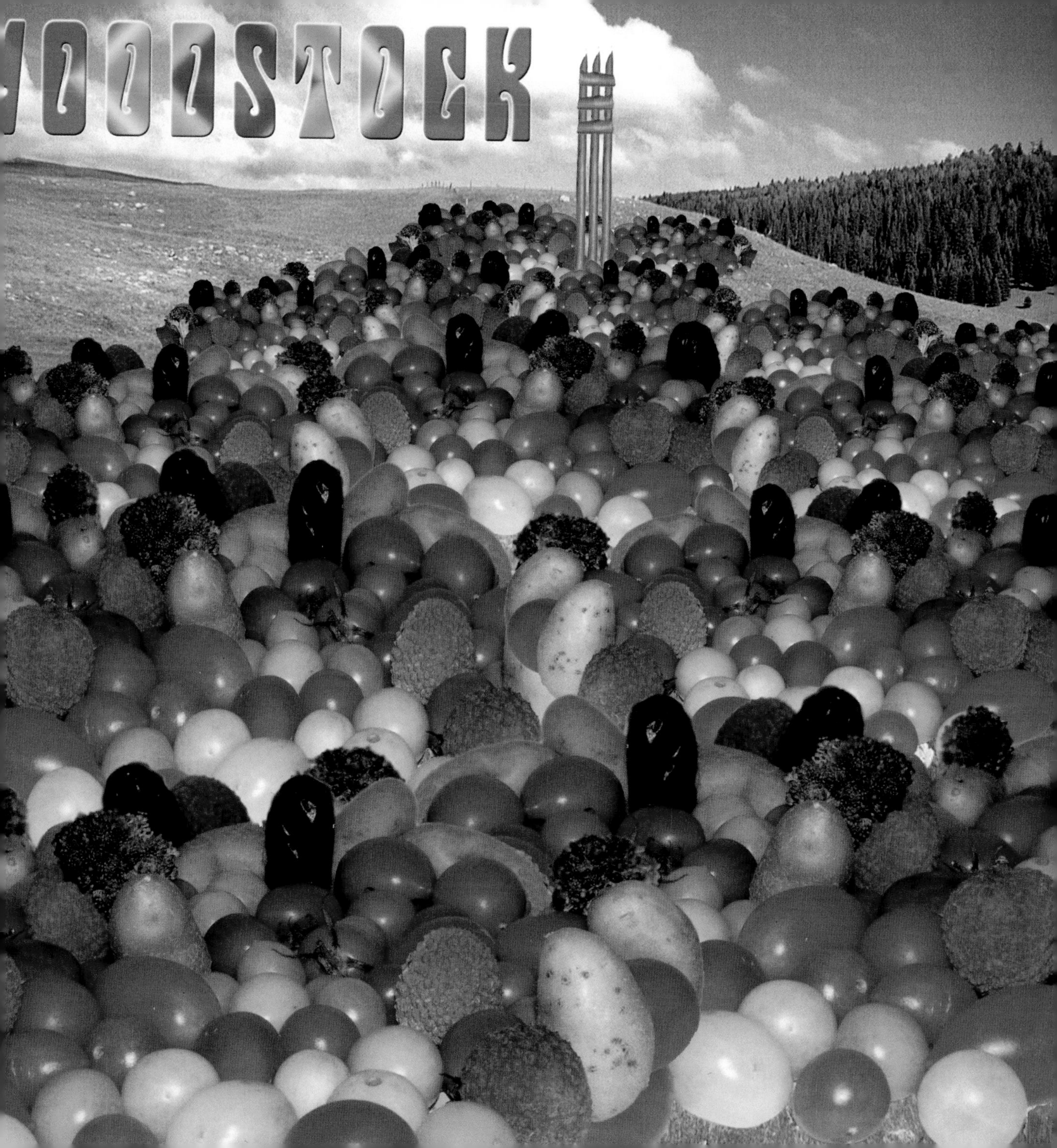
OODSTOCK

The Life and Times of Judge Roy Bean is released. Critics sniff.

Foreign Films

Foreign vegetables, much like many foreign films, are not so easily digestible in this country. While Americans will gobble up domestic classics such as *The Big Chili*, they are generally less interested in films or vegetables with unfamiliar-sounding names. Despite the critical acclaim of *Jean de (Broccoli) Florette*, the movie left a bitter taste with the American moviegoing public. And for the most part, foreign films in the United States never get to the suburban multiplex circuit. As one critic opined on their lack of success, "Americans want their movies and their vegetables presented the same way: simple, uncomplicated, and homegrown."

Losing Something in the Translation

For some reason, studios have difficulty translating foreign film titles that contain fruit or vegetable references. The following are both original and final translations of notable foreign films:

FILM: *Smultronstallet* (Sweden, 1957)
ORIGINAL TRANSLATION: *Strawberries Dance the Mambo Fast*
FINAL TRANSLATION: *Wild Strawberries*

FILM: *Mui Du Du Xanh* (Vietnam, 1993)
ORIGINAL TRANSLATION: *What Spoiled Fruit Smells Like*
FINAL TRANSLATION: *The Scent of Green Papaya*

FILM: *Xue Ying Han Mei* (Hong Kong, 1951)
ORIGINAL TRANSLATION: *Is That What I Think in the Snow?*
FINAL TRANSLATION: *Plum in the Snow*

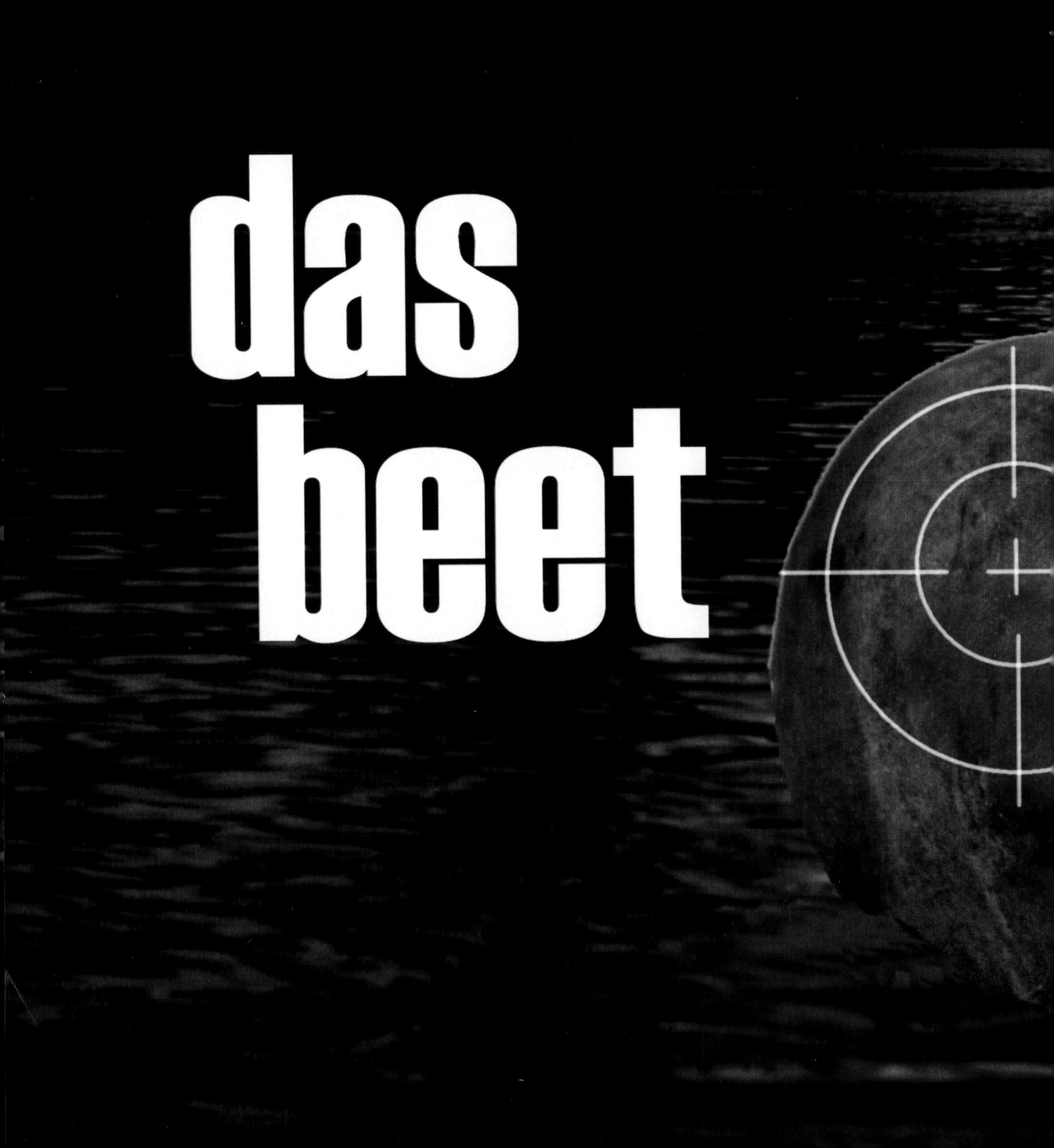
das
beet

Americans warmed to the universal theme of *Das Beet*, the story of a German submarine crew facing war, death, and, ultimately, borscht.

The Great Waldo Pepper is released. Critics sneeze.

Adult Cinema

From the early black-and-white smoker *Succ-o-tash* to the art house landmark *Last Mango in Paris*, the presence of fruits and vegetables in films has given new meaning to the term "skin trade." Early adult films (referred to as "peelers" in the industry) relied on a few lines of stilted dialogue ("Oh no, Mr. Root, not without a condiment!") before getting down to the action at hand. More often than not, the simple plot would revolve around a jumbo cucumber and some oversized casaba melons. A few simple scenes in the produce aisle—then "wham, bam, thank you, yam"—and the action would quickly move to the planting bed. The conclusion ("Oh my God, I'm cumin!") always featured the same predictable squishy result.

Debbie's problems begin when her boyfriend t
her to serve the salad undres

Blazing Saddles is released. Critics gasp.

As the adult movie business started to move more toward home videos ("take-outs," as the industry would call it), Hollywood found that there was a market for more subtle interpretations of eroticism. Adult films began to focus more on images such as freshly steamed ripe, young Brussels sprouts and would linger on scenes such as the long, slow basting of firm carrots with melted butter. The industry also began adding humor to many of its releases, including adult classics such as *Behind the Greengrocer's Door,* which offered up giggles with the pickles.

Up until thirty years ago, involving vegetables in the adult film industry required precision lockstep timing. One could measure in minutes the transition of a carrot from a firm, bright orange root to a drooping, spent noodle. Filming had to move quickly in order to take advantage of the freshness of the vegetables before the hot lights and passing time did their work. Then Tupperware was invented.

Close Encounters of the Third Kind is released. Sculpting mountains out of mashed potatoes becomes a minor fad in parts of the Midwest.

The industry hailed this amazing invention that could keep young vegetables fresh and firm for hours, days, even weeks. Celery stalks that browned and went limp after a five-minute session could look fresh even after five or six "salad tossings." Young sugar corn, which looked old and tired soon after its first shucking, suddenly made each shuck session look like the first time. And Tupperware resurrected the careers of more than a few vegetables that had seen their share of harvest moons since leaving the farm. A couple of hours of storage in this miracle plastic container after filming would keep the turnip that was previously destined for the stew pot performing like it had just been plucked from the rich, fertile earth. Truly an invention that saved the adult film industry.

Contemporary Cinema

The trend in recent years toward fresh, healthy vegetables has been mirrored in the film industry, where we see more and more vegetable content, or as the French call it, *l'influence legume*, in contemporary films. Are we becoming more focused on health and well-being, or do vegetables represent something more esoteric in our current world that we don't yet fully understand? Perhaps looking at a variety of recent films will help us to answer these questions.

The appeal of the Merchant-Ivory films to the aging baby boomer generation has mystified many industry wags. Some speculate that these producers have deftly wrapped classical themes in digestible presentations, packaging universal conflicts and issues with attractive

STAR WARS COLLECTIBLE # 35

YODA

STAR WARS COLLECTIBLE #193
JABBA THE HUTT

"May the borscht be with you."

The release of *Blade* marks the first film/consumer product co-branding from New Line Cinema and Henckels Knives.

young actors. But they miss the point: the attraction of films such as *Romaines of the Day*, *Howard's Endive*, and *Legume with a View* stems from their subliminal message that leafy roughage is the solution to many of life's problems.

With the close of a millennium and the beginning of a new, uncertain time, films are now focusing on a variety of issues that reflect society's attempts to cope in a perplexing and frightening world. Sexual confusion and ambiguous role models have been examined in both the *The Frying Game* and the hard-hitting *Boys Don't Fry*. End-of-century anxiety was paired with questionable food ingredients in the futuristic *Strange Glaze*. Even comedies have an edge to them in movies such as *Beet the Parents*, an exploration of modern family relationships, and *You've Got Kale*, a combination of Internet dating and home gardening.

this Hitchcock send-up, Mel Brooks displays how nausea can be duced by both vertigo and the smell of boiled cabbage.

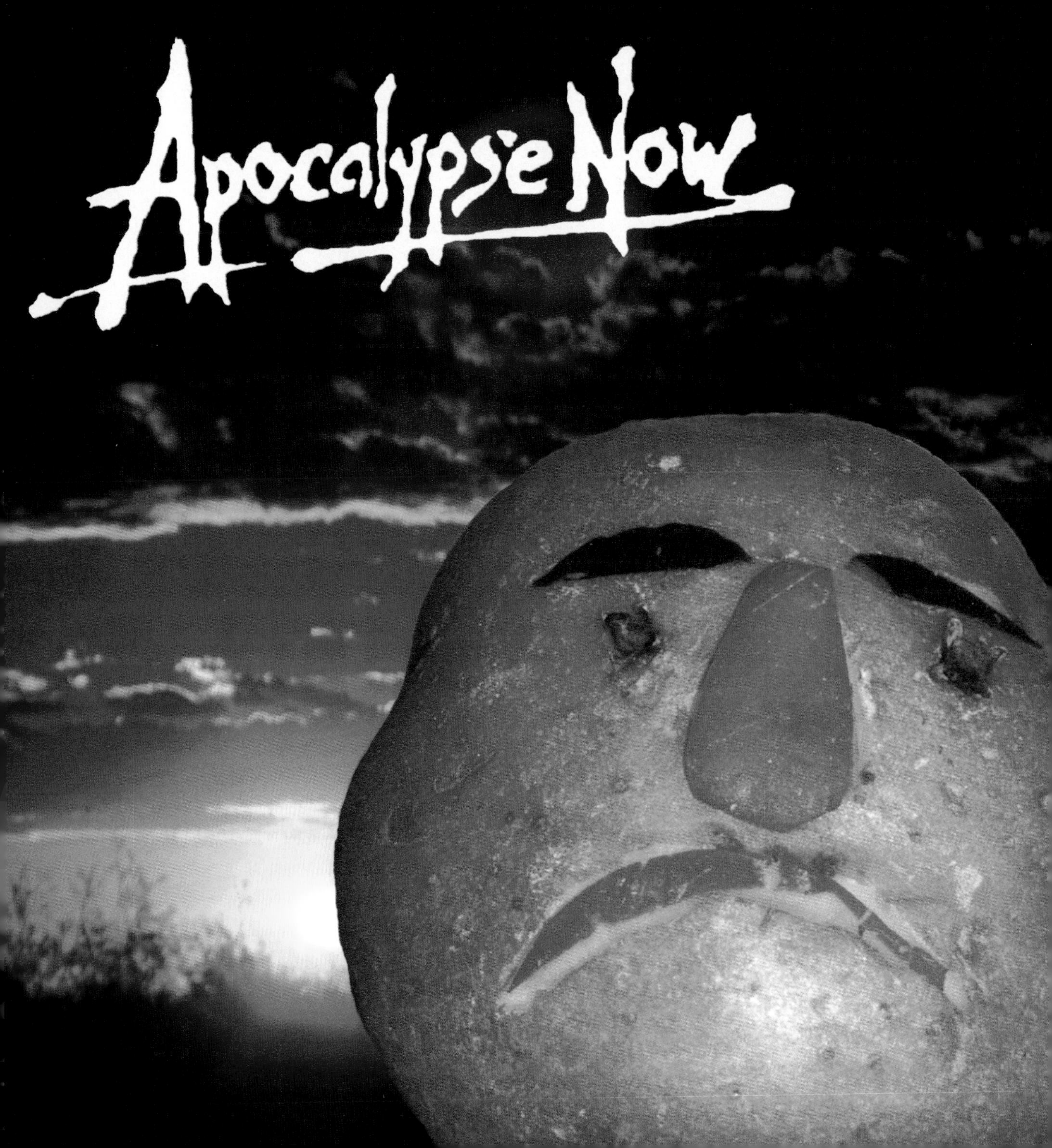
Apocalypse Now

Our Favorite Actors and Actresses

- Tim Curry

- Lara Flynn Boyle

- Peter Boyle

- Christina Pickle

- Barry Pepper

- Sean Bean

- Carrot Top

- Basil Rathbone

- Brad Pitt

A L I E N

"In space, no one can hear you steam .

"I am not an animal, I am a vegetable!"

The Green Team

The film world is well familiar with Albert "Cubby" Broccoli, the producer of many of James Bond's largest-grossing movies. But few know the story of how, in 1974, he recruited a young assistant producer named Alberto Celery, who had just completed work on Costa-Gavras's *State of Siege.* Cubby's vision was to create Broccoli-Celery Productions, a company that would produce vegetable-themed movies for filmgoers searching for lighter fare. He sensed that the public was growing tired of the meat-and-potatoes films of Charles Bronson and John Wayne and recognized the emerging economic power of the female audience and its desire for simply prepared plots with the dressing on the side.

The future seemed bright, but squabbles between the partners started. Celery immediately wanted to expand into foreign films and secretly hired Tim Curry for a project in India. When Broccoli found out he got steamed. Projects were stalled. The scent of shelved vegetable pictures began to chase away investors. The short-lived partnership ended in a mess. Broccoli went back to producing Bond movies and Celery got another assistant producer job. The sad story has been retold in a recently released short documentary, *Stalks and Bond: Why Two Green Vegetables Should Never Be Served Together.*

he original script portrayed the extra-terrestrial as an interstellar
oselytizer, attempting to convert the entire universe to a
getarian lifestyle. Originally titled *E.A.T.*, the movie fared poorly in
st screenings, so the outer space visitor was changed to a lost
tanist, and the title was shortened to *E.T.*

MISSISSIPPI BURNING

Tag Lines and Quotes We Would Like to See

- *Bananas*—"A film with unlimited appeal."

- *Beauty and the Beast*—"A tale as old as thyme"

- *The Fugitive*—"I did not grill my wife."

- *Field of Dreams*—"If you boiled it, they will come."

- *Gone with the Wind*—"Frankly my dear, I don't give a yam!"

- *King Kong*—"It was Beauty that dilled the beet."

ou can almost feel the heat of the Mississippi summer as the FBI
ashes with hooded chili peppers intent on keeping a "white
blano only" policy in their local groceries.

Remakes We Would Like to See

There are some movies, many classics in there own right, that just beg to be remade with a vegetable slant to the story. The following are movies we would like to see remade:

Bedtime for Garbonzo

Trouble ensues when Professor Peter Boyd, Jr., resurrects the "nature versus nurture" experiments his father conducted on a chimpanzee in the 1950s. This time around, however, rather than chimps, he focuses on the hibernation cycles of garbanzo beans.

The Black Scallion

Instead of a story about a horse, this remake focuses on a chef's attempts at combining Cajun and vegetarian cuisine.

Honey, I Blanched the Kids

Uh-oh! Dr. Wayne Szalinski is at it again, accidentally blanching his kids in one of his wayward hot tub inventions.

The Man Who Grew Too Much

The classic Hitchcock tale takes on a new twist with a story about a man who innocently grows too many tomatoes and finds himself entangled in a plot that includes blackmail, murder, and the Contadina family.

Pimento

An intricately plotted thriller that opens with a shot of a pimento-stuffed olive. As the plot-in-reverse unfolds, we get to see how the pimento gets stuffed. The film concludes with a shot of a glass jar of pimentos on the store shelf.

Silence of the Yams

Having tapped out on the cannibalism theme in *Hannibal*, the third encounter between Clarice Starling and Hannibal Lecter tells the sticky story of stockpiling sweet potatoes in a root cellar.

Texas Coleslaw Massacre, *starring Lettuce Head*

Unsuitable for the squeamish and the lactose intolerant, this groundbreaking brutal film introduces the Cuisinart as a murder weapon.

ney're mean, they're green, and they're overripe."   **The History of Hollywood in Vegetables**

The Ten Condiments

A fresh, vegetarian-inspired look at the Cecil B. DeMille classic:

1. I am ketchup, thy primary condiment. Thou shalt have no other tomato-based condiment before me.
2. Thou shalt not take the name of the Lord in vine.
3. Thou shalt not make unto thee any gravy image.
4. Remember the Sabbath day, for that is the day of the farmers' markets.
5. Honor thy father and mother, as well as thy grocer and gardener.
6. Thou shalt not dill, except in the case of cucumbers and young tomatoes.
7. Thou shalt not commit adultery, no matter how much thou might relish the opportunity.
8. Thou shalt not steal, but it is okay to taste a grape or two in the produce aisle.
9. Thou shalt not bear false hummus.
10. Thou shalt not covet thy neighbor's garden, no matter how juicy the tomatoes look.

_a_ **STAR** _is_ **CORN**

Kevin discovers the worst part about being left home alone: having to eat his leftover brussels sprou

HOME  ALONe

The Blair Witch Projec

The Greatest Vegetable Movie Never Seen

One of the greatest vegetable films ever produced was never released for commercial distribution and never even released on videotape. The movie, *Veg-O-Matic*, tells the story of the psychological undoing of Ron Popeil, the inventor of the infamous household appliance of the same name. Tracing Ron's early leanings, eagerly helping his mother grate carrots for family dinners, the film follows his determination to patent first the Veg-O-Matic and the subsequent, even ghastlier, Juice-O-Matic. The film concludes by examining Mr. Popeil's current existence as a wealthy retiree, haunted by the horrors of his past deeds.

October of 1994, three student filmmakers disappeared in the
ods near Burkittesville, Maryland, while shooting a
cumentary. A year later only seeds and rind were found.

The infamous Dr. Evil's pinky-sucking pose was originally an off-camera attempt by Mike Myers to dislodge a stubborn kernel of corn wedged in his molar.

DINOSAUR

When herbivores roamed the earth.

GRUMPY
OLD MEN

These vegetables have been down in the cellar for quite some time.

INDEPENDENCE DAY

July 2nd they arrive, July 3rd they attack, July 4th is Independence Day, and July 5th they are blanched.

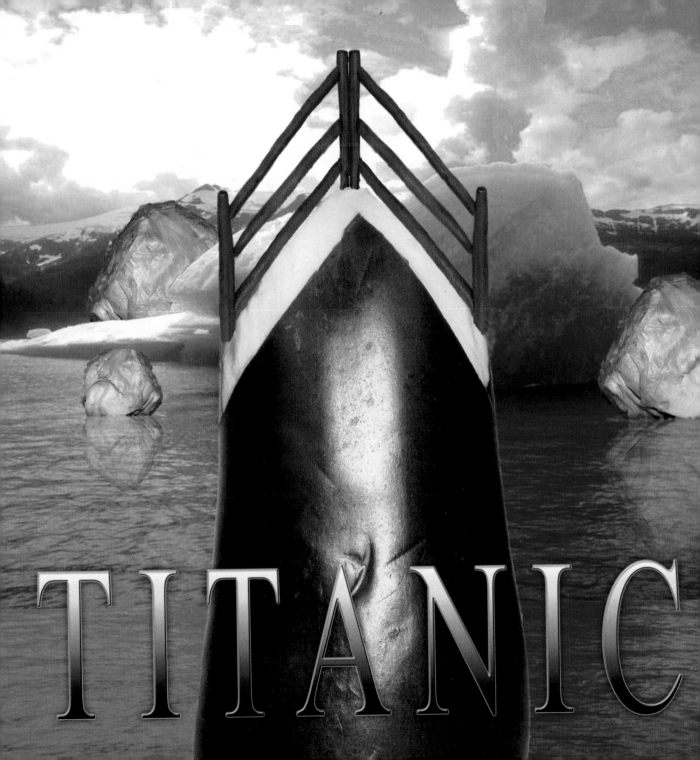

Tobey Maguire and Natalie Portman named Sexiest Vegetarians of the Year by PETA.

Coming Attractions

So where do vegetables in films go from here? It is encouraging to see that current movies such as *Wallace and Grommit: The Great Vegetable Plot* and *Pumpkin* are not afraid to come right out with the vegetable name—a trend seen in earlier films such as *One Potato, Two Potato; Fried Green Tomatoes;* and *Children of the Corn.* I am also optimistic about the fact that recent movies reflect the wide-ranging influence of vegetables in the industry. From the G-rated family film *Soy Story* to the teenage classic *Dude, Where's My Cardamom,* to adult-themed movies such as the Oscar-winning *A Beautiful Rind,* it is clear that the vegetable-film link has deep roots. While it would be difficult to speculate on what the coming years may bring to the screen, one thing is for certain: the marriage of celluloid and celery will last well into the future.

MONSTERS, INC

Chapter Three

How to Make a Vegetable Sculpture

So You Want to Play with Your Food?

Appreciating this book's vegetable art and play on words is one thing. Making the decision to take paring knife in hand and start sculpting is a much greater endeavor. Before you make your final decision, ask yourself, "Do I really want to be known to my friends as someone whose artistic impulses are manifested through onion peels and broccoli stalks?" If the answer is yes, and you make a committment to the craft, your life will change in both subtle and not so subtle ways. You will smile appreciatively as you receive the inevitable cucumber tie, artichoke earrings, or carrot boxer shorts. You will find you have become a very popular invitee to Oscar-night parties, always asked to bring the centerpiece. And, as the appetizer tray is passed your way, you will wince with each "can-of-peas" joke you hear.

But your life will also start to change in distinctly positive

ways. You will become friendly with the produce people at your local supermarket, chatting about shipment dates and bemoaning dock tie-ups. You'll change your computer's homepage from msnbc.com to producepete.com. You will tune in to your local radio station on Saturday mornings to hear the greengrocer's report. And you will begin to understand fully the humanity of Cesar Chavez.

If you've taken all of this into consideration and your desire to sculpt is still strong, some preparation for your sojourn into this new world is in order. This section will show you how to plan your work, discuss important issues to consider in designing your sculptures, provide recommendations on the best tools to use for sculpting, tell you what to look for when shopping for vegetables, teach you the ins and outs of the sculpting process, and, finally, give you advice on how to store and transport your creations.

But once you have made the commitment, it is a short step from carving Woody Allen out of a turnip to chairing activities for your local chapter of PETA (People for the Ethical Treatment of Artichokes). Don't say you haven't been warned.

Planning Your Work

Every good vegetable project begins with a plan. You obviously have your own personal reasons for wanting to create a particular movie-themed vegetable sculpture. Perhaps you're planning a party and want to impress your friends with your wit and creativity. Or you want to surprise a movie-loving coworker with a unique birthday gift. Maybe you are just tired of watching the *Late Show* by yourself and want to create a low-calorie companion to snack on during commercials.

Whatever ideas you come up with, remember that successful sculpting always involves three critical elements: **P**resentation, **E**xecution, and **A**ppropriateness—what I call the principles of the **PEA.**

The *presentation* of your sculpture is a particularly significant part of the planning process. The appropriate *tableau* for the creation must carefully be considered. More than likely your sculpture will be part of a larger presentation, perhaps a centerpiece on a table or a focal point

for a basket of crudités. You'll need to think beyond the sculpture itself and consider the full arrangement. For example, you might surround your *Lawrence of Arabia* sculpture with dry grits to simulate desert sand. Or what better to encircle a creation of Hannibal Lecter with than fresh fava beans? Using your wit and imagination in the presentation will make a big difference in the final product.

Just as *execution* in non-vegetable films can mean the difference between a Palme d'Or winner at Cannes and a straight-to-video release, execution is all-important in the food sculpting business as well. The quality of the tools, the freshness of the vegetables, and the close attention to small details (those coriander seed earrings are the finishing touch to Holly Go-Lightly's outfit) all contribute to a successful sculpture.

Finally, *appropriateness* of the vegetables selected for a sculpture must reflect that particular movie's theme, genre, and era. Nothing would look sillier than a sculpture of the 1950s classic *The Sweet Smell of Lettuce* made from nineties ingredients such as arugula and radicchio.

Designing Your Sculpture

Once you settle on an idea, the next step is to make a sketch of that idea. Don't worry if your artistic skills are one notch below a third-grader. Putting your idea down on paper will help you visualize the piece.

In the design stage you don't need to attempt an exact replication of an actor or a movie image. If sculpting is new to you, trying to re-create Marilyn Monroe in *The Seven Year Itch* may be too much too soon. Rather, you simply might want to re-create the subway grate scene with an onion skin skirt and two shapely carrots for Marilyn's legs. As your skills progress, you can have a go at more complicated projects. And try not to overuse one type of vegetable in the design. Contrast and variety make the sculpture more visually interesting.

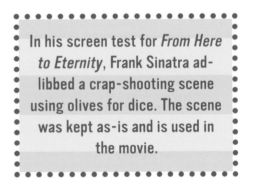

In his screen test for *From Here to Eternity*, Frank Sinatra ad-libbed a crap-shooting scene using olives for dice. The scene was kept as-is and is used in the movie.

boiling onion   tomato   new potato   heads

eggplant   squash   cucumber   bodies

Vegetable proportions.

As you design your sculpture, think about the relative sizes of the vegetables that you will be using. Since you won't know the exact size and shape of each piece until after you have shopped, leave some room for error in your designs. You will find that round or oval vegetables such as onions or potatoes make excellent heads. Squash and eggplant are good choices for bodies, as they sculpt easily and most of them are torso-shaped. If your sculpture is going to be a person, the head should be about a quarter of the size of the body. Arms and legs can be tricky—asparagus spears, carrot or celery slices, or split cucumbers work well. Don't get too fancy with appendages (unless your sculpture is the giant squid from *20,000 Leeks Under the Sea*). Vegetable arms and legs tend to overcomplicate the sculptures and usually end up resembling prosthetic devices, a look that I doubt you would like to achieve.

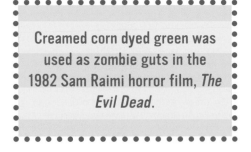

Creamed corn dyed green was used as zombie guts in the 1982 Sam Raimi horror film, *The Evil Dead*.

The most important part of your sculpture will generally be the face. Whether it is that steely glare from Arnold Schwarzenegger or a come-hither glance from Marlene Dietrich that you are trying to evoke, the materials you select for the face are crucial. There are a number of options for the eyes. Cloves that retain the "star" collar are excellent to use for women's eyes. They invoke a wide-eyed innocence—think of the young Goldie Hawn. A wide range of beans or peas, some with markings that resemble pupils, can be used to excellent effect.

a STAR *is* CORN

Consider using black-eyed peas, French lentils, or split peas. But sometimes a simple knife slit will be sufficient to indicate something like a Clint Eastwood–type squint. Having trouble with Woody Allen's face? Try using round radish or cucumber slices for his glasses. The shape or contour of some vegetables may suggest eyes without any further sculpting. Remember, the simpler the better.

Veggie Tales: Dave and the Giant Pickle (1996) is the biblical story of David and Goliath told in vegetables.

The simplicity rule holds true particularly for the nose. Look to use vegetables such as small peppers with natural "noses" suggested by their shape. If you are going for a different look, small carrot slices will do justice to any Beverly Hills plastic surgeon's creation. For a more ethnic look, you might want to try portions of a baby carrot, red pepper, or even raw ginger. Experiment a little before making your final rhinoplastic decision.

The mouth can be tricky, so your attention to detail here is critical. Crescent-shape slices from a large radish work well for relatively simple mouths. A second cutout inside the slice will imply an open mouth—

cut small notch for a mouth

perfect for that Martha Raye figure you're planning. A round radish slice for the mouth will give your sculpture a look of surprise. You may want to get a bit more adventurous and use kernels of corn or uncooked rice as teeth. If you are using corn, it's best to boil the corn and then refrigerate it for at least three hours prior to sculpting. The kernels can then be removed in nice even rows, perfect for displaying that dazzling Tom Cruise smile. Again, be daring—a pointed daikon root dripping with beet juice would scare me as much as an encounter with the real Dracula.

Like mouths, ears also can be difficult. Using your vegetable's natural shapes is the least obtrusive way to go and therefore is your best bet. Unless you are sculpting Mickey Mouse or Alfalfa from the *Our Gang* comedies, my advice is to go easy on the ears.

Leafy legumes such as lettuce, parsley, or purple cabbage are excellent to use for hair. Curly hair may be created with long carrot or cucumber peels. If you are going for that sparse, white-haired Walter Brennan coif, you can use the semi-transparent outer skin of a white onion to crown the head.

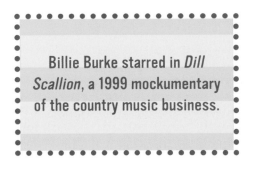

Billie Burke starred in *Dill Scallion*, a 1999 mockumentary of the country music business.

Finally, remember that all your sculptures won't necessarily be humans. Look beyond the obvious when you're designing your sculpture. How about a bunch of little Brussels sprouts marines to portray *Guadalcanal Diary*? Or a sea of flying portobello mushrooms for *Independence Day*? The best tool at your—pardon the expression—disposal is your imagination.

How to Make a Vegetable Sculpture

Using the Right Tools

In the sculpting business we like to use the expression "The right tool for the right cob." That is, the most important ingredient in a successful vegetable creation is the proper set of tools, and many of these tools may already be in your kitchen drawers. Start with the basics and, as you become more adept and adventurous, add new tools as you see fit.

You'll need to start with three basic knives: a three-and-a-half-inch paring knife, a medium-size knife with a six-inch blade, and a large knife with a ten-inch blade. Do not use blades with serrated edges or any other cutting tool that tears rather than slices. It is critical that you keep your knives sharp, so purchasing a six-inch sharpening stone is a wise investment for the serious sculptor. Use the paring knife for all your detail work such as carving the features of the face. The six-inch knife is used for general work such as preparing, shaping, and slicing the vegetables. The ten-inch knife should be used for cutting down large vegetables.

Knives should be sufficient for almost all of your basic sculpting needs. But you might want to include a vegetable peeler (very handy for making long, curly hair), a lemon zester, and a vegetable slicer in your sculpting kit. For the experienced sculptor, the biggest advantage of an extensive set of sculpting tools is the impressive looks you get when you whip them out at a gathering to put the finishing touches to your creation. Just don't let your audience know that you are really using only one knife to finish the sculpture.

Shopping for Vegetables

You will discover that your grocery shopping chores, once a simple afternoon errand, will become much more complicated. The best thing to do is to shop at two different local markets. The first can be your standard grocery store, assuming it stocks fresh produce and is reasonably priced. Any large chain supermarket will do. This is where you should get all your standard items—eggplant, cabbage, corn, and the like. You will also need to find a gourmet store that carries specialty items that are not usually found at large grocers. In the New York/Connecticut area, I prefer Balducci's and Hay Day markets for their selection and quality of produce. For more exotic sculptures, seek out local ethnic markets. A journey to a Chinatown grocery will yield unique vegetables that you never heard of before. The white asparagus that you are using for Ionic columns in your *Hercules Unchained* sculpture just cannot be found at the local A&P. It's also a good idea to get to know the manager of the produce department at

a STAR *is* CORN

your local gourmet store—he or she just might be able to find you that crucial out-of-season lychee nut for your *It Came from Outer Space* sculpture.

Do not think it strange when you catch yourself foraging through the potato bin to find the perfect spud for your *Rocky* sculpture. And if you are patient and take the time to look at your vegetables from more than one angle, you will discover more actors' faces than there are in the Academy Players Directory. Just try to control your enthusiasm when you discover a head of cauliflower that is a dead ringer for Margaret Dumont. (A little hint—not everyone will share your excitement.)

Make sure to leave plenty of extra time at the checkout counter. As the typical cashier will be unfamiliar with certain exotic vegetables in your basket, it may take longer to check out than to pass through security at the Athens airport. It's a good idea to take note of the item name and price per pound when you are shopping so that when your cashier raises his or her eyebrows in confusion, you can jump in with "Salsify, $7.99 a pound!"

Sculpting

Once your design is completed and you have done all your shopping, you are ready to work on your masterpiece. Find a quiet place in your home that is removed from household activity. You should set up two adjacent work surfaces—your sculpting surface plus an area to lay out your vegetables, tools, and accessories. (Make sure the surface is high enough so it is out of reach of curious toddlers or hungry pets—Morgan Freeman's head once served as a light snack for our golden retriever). Your sculpting area should be well lit and your cutting board should be durable and of sufficient size to handle large projects.

Before you begin, you will need to figure out the timing of the individual components of your project. As a general rule, you should begin your sculpture no more than three hours before presentation. Certain vegetables, such as eggplants, brown relatively quickly once their flesh is exposed to air. While this browning can be retarded with lemon juice (which you should keep nearby in a bowl with a small brush), you gener-

ally want to carve these items last so they will look their freshest when the sculpture is presented. Also, once any vegetable has been cut or pierced, it will begin to dry out and shrink. This is important to remember when you are carving small features like mouths or eyes for which you might want to place a small item in a carved-out portion of a larger vegetable. There is nothing more embarrassing than to proudly place your sculpture of Sammy Davis, Jr., in the center of the table and then watch while his only eye drops out and rolls onto the floor.

The more complex portions of the sculpture—usually the head or the face—should be completed first. If you make a mistake at this point,

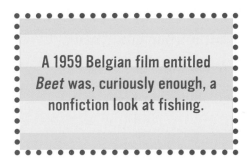

A 1959 Belgian film entitled *Beet* was, curiously enough, a nonfiction look at fishing.

you can start over without worrying about the body—the larger portion of the sculpture—sitting around and drying out. Once you have completed the individual portions of the sculpture, you can wrap them with wet paper towels and refrigerate them if necessary. Keeping cut vegetables away from air and heat will preserve the life and freshness of your sculpture.

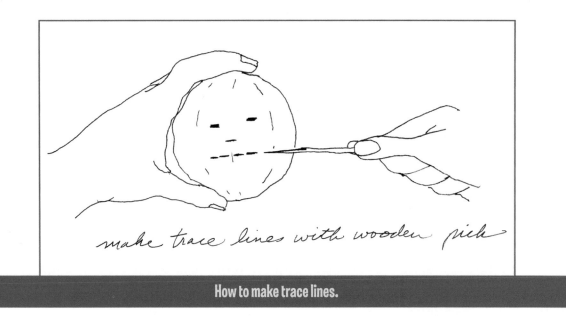

make trace lines with wooden pick

How to make trace lines.

Bring your vegetables to room temperature before you begin sculpting. This will give you greater control over your cuts. Again, make sure your knives are very sharp. Start your sculpture by tracing very light strokes over the portions of the vegetables that you will be carving. These trace lines should be heavy enough so they can be used as guides. Start your carving with small cuts and strokes. You can always go back and make them larger if necessary. Your knife strokes should be even and smooth, using a gentle but firm sawing motion.

Never rotate your knife or force a cut, as this may cause you to lose control of the cutting motion and potentially waste a lot of hard work.

The simplest way of fastening or attaching the components of your sculpture is to carve out pieces of the larger vegetable and to place the eyes, mouths, or other features in these indentations. At times you will need to attach two or more elements in a more secure

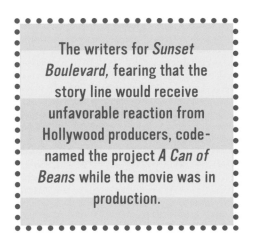

The writers for *Sunset Boulevard*, fearing that the story line would receive unfavorable reaction from Hollywood producers, code-named the project *A Can of Beans* while the movie was in production.

manner. Toothpicks and bamboo skewers are the perfect tools for this task. When attaching pieces, always use two picks, evenly spaced apart. This will prevent the attached piece from rotating or drooping. Wooden skewers work well for larger operations such as attaching a head to a body or for giving a structural "spine" to your sculpture.

Remember to keep extra toothpicks handy should your figure start to loosen around the picks already in place. Using a fast-stick adhesive such as Krazy Glue can occasionally work for attaching small facial

How to Make a Vegetable Sculpture

items or strands of hair to a figure. Sculpture purists may frown on this on the grounds that it violates the principle of using only natural materials. But let's get serious here—would you rather have a handsome creation or take advice from someone who considers himself a sculpture purist?

Transporting and Storing Your Sculpture

More often than not you will be transporting your vegetable creations, perhaps bringing them to a party. Careful planning will assure that your sculptures are presented in the freshest state possible. Pack wet paper towels, extra toothpicks, a small water sprayer, a plastic bag of ice, and your set of carving tools. If you have a long ride ahead of you, you should consider doing the final assembly after you arrive, especially for delicate items such as arms and legs. Before you leave home, carefully wrap the individual vegetable components in wet paper towels. And wrap the carved pieces that have a tendency to brown quickly (carved eggplant, for example) in paper towels soaked in lemon juice. Place the items in a box cushioned

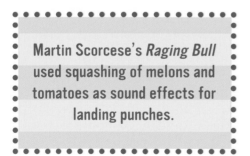

Martin Scorcese's *Raging Bull* used squashing of melons and tomatoes as sound effects for landing punches.

with some padding such as wadded newspaper or bunched towels. And finally, get used to that onion smell in your car—it is the mark of honor of an expert sculptor.

When you arrive at your destination, find a quiet, isolated area to complete your work. Check your sculpture for areas that have dried out or connections that may have loosened. If necessary, reset toothpick connectors in freshly placed holes to assure a more secure fit. Once your project is completely assembled, give your vegetables a quick spray of water to freshen them. Then proudly present your figure to an admiring crowd.

The model for the *Millennium Falcon* in *Star Wars* was a hamburger with a large, round olive at its side.

Sculptures will generally last about three hours before they start to droop and degrade. Figures composed of more delicate items such as lettuce will become limp more quickly. If you are brave, you might want to time your sculpture of Marie Antoinette so that her head topples off her body just as your party reaches its peak.

Closing Credits

The following is a list of the vegetables used for the sculptures in order of appearance:

Gene Shallot (PAGE IV)

Shallot (for the head)

Radish (for the eyeglasses)

Carrot (for the nose and bowtie)

French lentil (for the eyes and the dot in the bowtie)

Eggplant (for body, eyebrows, mustache)

Romaine lettuce (for the hair)

Saul (Solly G) Goldberg (PAGE XII)

Honeydew melon (for the head)

Italian pepper (for the nose)

Carrot (for the cigar butt)

Corn (for the teeth)

Black beans (for the eyes)

Charlie Chaplin (PAGE 4)

- Eggplant (for the body, mouth, eyebrows, derby, and tie)
- White onion (for the head; root of onion for the mustache)
- Carrot (for the nose)
- Cloves (for the eyes)
- Skin from russet potato (for the hair)

The Invisible Man (PAGE 7)

- White onion (for the head)
- Eggplant (for the body, tie, sunglasses, and hat)

The Grapes of Wrath (PAGE 9)

- Red and green grapes (for the heads)
- Radish (for the mouths, noses, and glasses)
- Split peas (for some of the eyes and noses)
- French lentils (for some of the eyes)

Pinocchio (PAGE 10)

- Golden beet (for the head)
- Radish (for the mouth)
- Black-eyed peas (for the eyes)
- Red pepper (for the hat)

The Sands of Iwo Jima (PAGE 12)
- Buckwheat groats (for the sand)
- Tomatillos (for the Marines)
- Carrot (for the flagpole)
- Fig (for the flag)

The Day the Earth Stood Still (PAGE 15)
- Yellow squash (for the body)
- Gingerroot (for the head)
- French lentils (for the eyes, nose, and pendant)

Buttersquash 8 (PAGE 16)
- Butternut squash (for the body)
- Yellow onion (for the head)
- Radish (for the mouth)
- Carrot (for the nose)
- French lentils (for the eyes)
- Purple cabbage (for the hair)
- Endive (for the slip)
- Eggplant (for the eyebrows)

Psycho (PAGE 18)
- Garnet yam (for the arm)
- Carrot (for the knife)
- Nori seaweed (for the shower curtain)

The Graduate (PAGE 21)
- Holland eggplant (for the graduate's body and mortarboard)
- Mushroom (for the graduate's head)
- Jewel yam (for Mrs. Robinson's leg)
- French lentils (for the eyes)
- Radish (for the mouth)

Woodstock (PAGE 23)
- Cherry tomatoes
- Fingerling potatoes
- Broccoli
- Lychee nuts
- Medjool dates
- *Haricot verts* (for the tower)

Das Beet (PAGES 26–27)
- Red beet (for the sub)

Debbie Does Salad (PAGE 29)
- White onion (for the head)
- Cloves (for the eyes)
- Carrot (for the nose)
- French lentil (for the birthmark)
- Radish (for the mouth)
- Frisée lettuce (for the hair)
- Large white onions (for body and breasts)

Jaws (PAGE 33)
- Daikon root (for the body)
- Cloves (for the eyes)

Yoda (PAGE 34)
- Winter squash (for the head)
- Endive (for the ears)
- French lentils (for the eyes)

Jabba the Hutt (PAGE 35)
- Squash (for the head)
- French lentils (for the eyes)

High Anxiety (PAGE 36)
- Red onion (for the vortex)
- Sculpted carrot sticks (for the body)

Apocalypse Now (PAGE 38)
- Red potato (for the head)
- Eggplant (for the eyebrows)
- Radish (for the nose and mouth)

Alien (PAGE 40)
- Cactus pear (for the head)
- Arborio rice (for the teeth)
- French lentil (for the eyes)

Closing Credits

The Elephant Man (PAGE 41)

Japanese eggplant (for the body and hat)

Elephant garlic—what else? (for the head)

Cloves (for the eyes and shirt buttons)

Blanched scallion green (for the scarf)

E.T. (PAGE 42)

French lentil (for the nostrils)

Black bean (for the eyes)

Celery root (for the head)

Parsnip (for the body)

Mississippi Burning (PAGE 44)

White poblano chili peppers (for the bodies)

French lentils (for the eyes)

Teenage Mutant Ninja Turtles (PAGE 46)

Heirloom green tomato (for the head)

Black-eyed peas (for the eyes)

Home Alone (PAGE 49)

Boiling onion (for the head)

Frisée lettuce (for the hair)

- Radish (for the mouth)
- Black-eyed peas (for the eyes)
- Carrot (for the nose and hands)

The Blair Witch Project (PAGE 50)

- Butternut squash (for the face and nose)
- Winter squash (for the knit cap)
- Carrot sticks (for the stick doll figure)

Dr. Evil (PAGE 52)

- Honeydew melon (for the head)
- Black beans (for the eyes)
- Radish (for the mouth)
- Carrot (for the nose and hand)
- Eggplant (for the eyebrows)

Dinosaur (PAGE 53)

- Garnet yam (for the dinosaur)

Grumpy Old Men (PAGE 54)

- Chayote (for the heads)
- Black beans (for one set of eyes)
- Black-eyed peas (for the other set of eyes)
- French lentils (for the nose of one)
- Carrot (for the nose of the other)
- Winter squash (for the bodies)

Independence Day (PAGE 55)

- Portobello mushroom (for the alien spacecraft)

Titanic (PAGE 56)

- Eggplant (for the ship)
- *Haricot verts* (for the ship's rail)
- Iceberg lettuce (for the you-know-whats)

Monsters, Inc. (PAGE 58)

- Lemon (for the body)
- Black-eyed pea (for the eye)

Closing Credits

About the Author

This is Paul Eagle's first book, written under the *nom legume* of Brock Lee. Paul first became attracted to vegetables at an early age. His first sculpture, an homage to a bald neighbor, was a pair of sunglasses strategically placed on a honeydew melon. While his friends were playing Little League baseball, Paul would stake out farmers' markets. In junior high, he volunteered for duty in the school cafeteria, amusing both classmates and faculty with carrot stick figurines of his gym teacher. His thematic sculpture for the high school prom, *Bridge over Troubled Watercress*, was a major hit.

Eventually Paul traded in his carving knife for a T square and pursued formal training in architecture. After many successful years in the field, Paul is still drawn to the art of the carved vegetable. *A Star Is Corn* has put Paul back in his natural medium.

Paul currently lives in Weston, Connecticut, with his wife, two children, and dog. They are strict non-vegetarians.